TRAGEDY! TALES FROM THE TITANIC

Disaster Strikes!

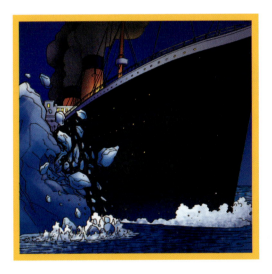

BY SARAH EASON
ILLUSTRATED BY ALBERTO SAICHANN

BEARPORT PUBLISHING
Minneapolis, Minnesota

BEAR CLAW

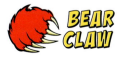

Credits

20, © Wikimedia Commons/SeichanGant; 21t, © Alamy/Science History Images; 21b, © Wikimedia Commons/L. P. Skidmore; 22t, © United States Library of Congress; 22b, © Wikimedia Commons; 23, © Wikimedia Commons/The Graphic.

Editor: Jennifer Sanderson
Proofreader: Katie Dicker
Designer: Paul Myerscough
Picture Researcher: Katie Dicker

Bearport Publishing Company Product Development Team

Publisher: Jen Jenson; Director of Product Development: Spencer Brinker; Managing Editor: Allison Juda; Editor: Cole Nelson; Associate Editor: Naomi Reich; Associate Editor: Tiana Tran; Art Director: Colin O'Dea; Designer: Kim Jones; Designer: Kayla Eggert; Product Development Specialist: Owen Hamlin

Statement on Usage of Generative Artificial Intelligence

Bearport Publishing remains committed to publishing high-quality nonfiction books. Therefore, we restrict the use of generative AI to ensure accuracy of all text and visual components pertaining to a book's subject. See BearportPublishing.com for details.

A Note on Graphic Narrative Nonfiction

This graphic story is a dramatization based on true events. It is intended to give the reader a sense of the narrative rather than a presentation of actual details as they occurred.

Library of Congress Cataloging-in-Publication Data

Names: Eason, Sarah, author. | Saichann, Alberto, illustrator.
Title: Disaster strikes! / Sarah Eason ; Illustrated by Alberto Saichann.
Description: Bear claw books. | Minneapolis, Minnesota : Bearport Publishing Company, [2025] | Series: Tragedy! Tales from the Titanic | Includes bibliographical references and index.
Identifiers: LCCN 2024034192 (print) | LCCN 2024034193 (ebook) | ISBN 9798892328562 (library binding) | ISBN 9798892329460 (paperback) | ISBN 9798892328630 (ebook)
Subjects: LCSH: Titanic (Steamship)--Juvenile literature. | Titanic (Steamship)--Comic books, strips, etc. | Ocean liners--Great Britain--History--20th century--Juvenile literature. | Ocean liners--Great Britain--History--20th century--Comic books, strips, etc. | Shipwrecks--North Atlantic Ocean--History--20th century--Juvenile literature. | Shipwrecks--North Atlantic Ocean--History--20th century--Comic books, strips, etc. | Graphic novels.
Classification: LCC G530.T6 E26 2025 (print) | LCC G530.T6 (ebook) | DDC 910.9163/4--dc23/eng20240724
LC record available at https://lccn.loc.gov/2024034192
LC ebook record available at https://lccn.loc.gov/2024034193

Copyright © 2025 Bearport Publishing Company. All rights reserved. No part of this publication may be reproduced in whole or in part, stored in any retrieval system, or transmitted in any form or by any means, electronic, mechanical, photocopying, recording, or otherwise, without written permission from the publisher.

For more information, write to Bearport Publishing, 5357 Penn Avenue South, Minneapolis, MN 55419.

Contents

CHAPTER 1
A Floating Palace 4

CHAPTER 2
Disaster Strikes 8

CHAPTER 3
Nightmare at Sea 14

The Sinking of the *Titanic* 20
More *Titanic* Stories 22
Glossary 23
Index 24
Read More 24
Learn More Online 24

CHAPTER 1

A Floating Palace

RMS *Titanic* set off for its first journey on April 10, 1912. It was the largest ship in the world and designed to be one of the most **opulent** passenger ships ever built.

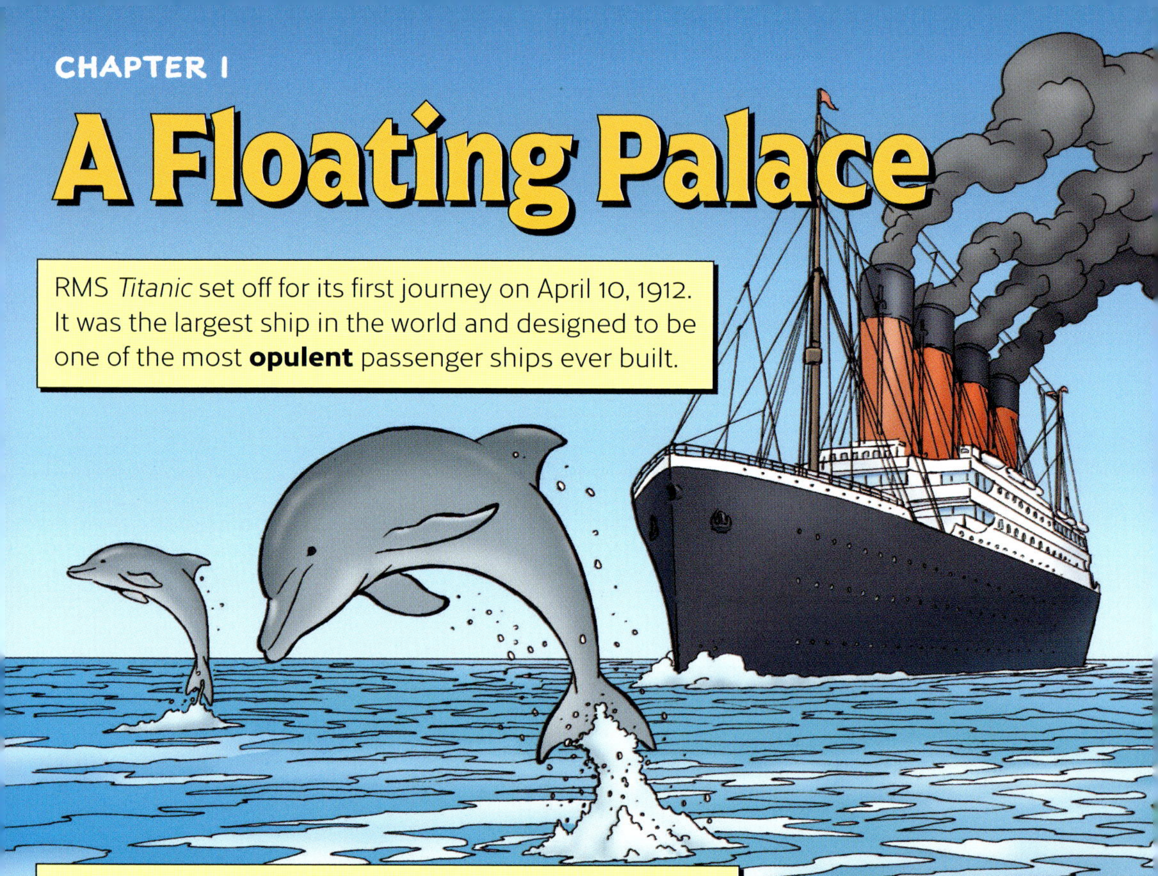

As *Titanic* sped across the Atlantic, first-class passengers enjoyed **luxuries** such as a pool, gym, and spa.

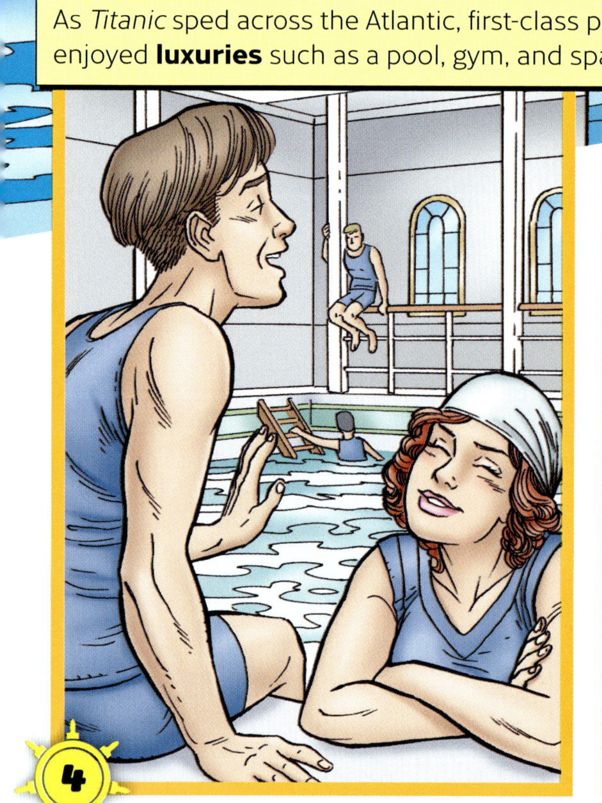

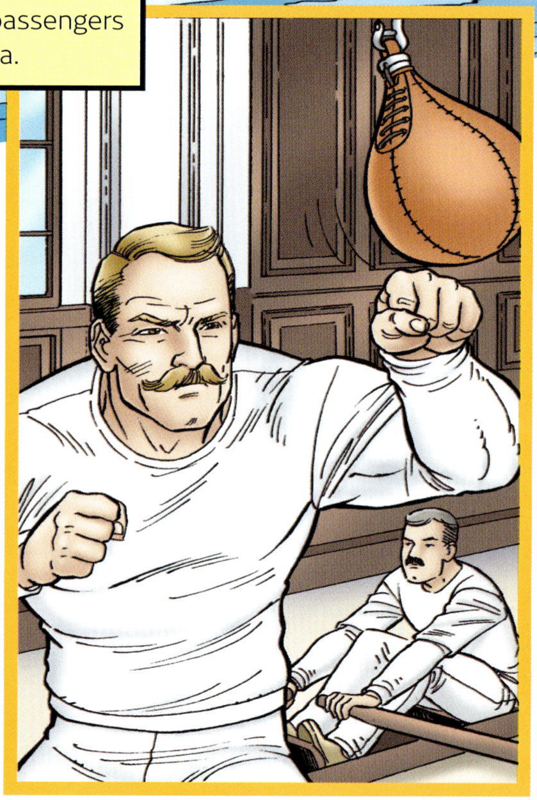

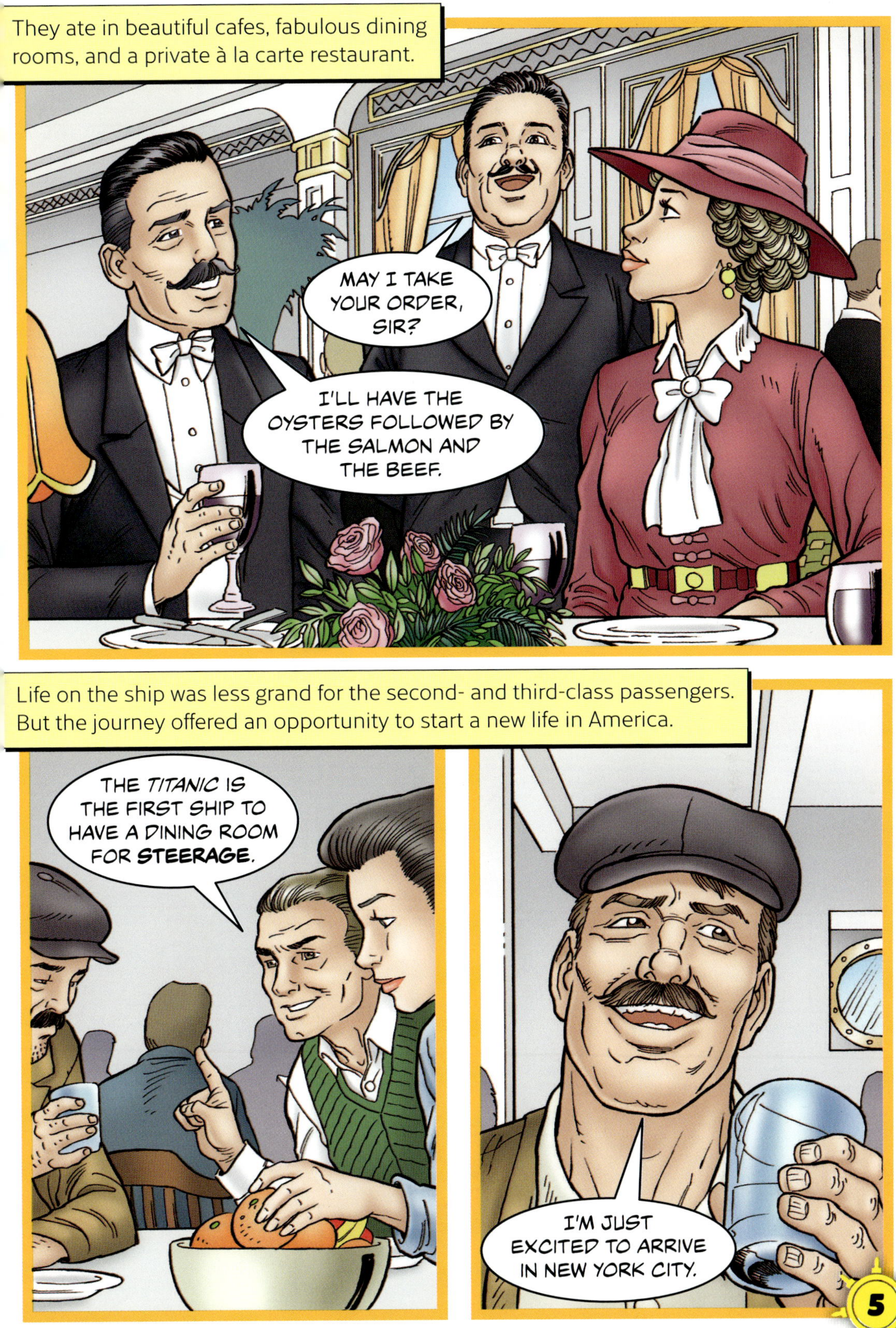
They ate in beautiful cafes, fabulous dining rooms, and a private à la carte restaurant.
MAY I TAKE YOUR ORDER, SIR?
I'LL HAVE THE OYSTERS FOLLOWED BY THE SALMON AND THE BEEF.
Life on the ship was less grand for the second- and third-class passengers. But the journey offered an opportunity to start a new life in America.
THE *TITANIC* IS THE FIRST SHIP TO HAVE A DINING ROOM FOR **STEERAGE**.
I'M JUST EXCITED TO ARRIVE IN NEW YORK CITY.

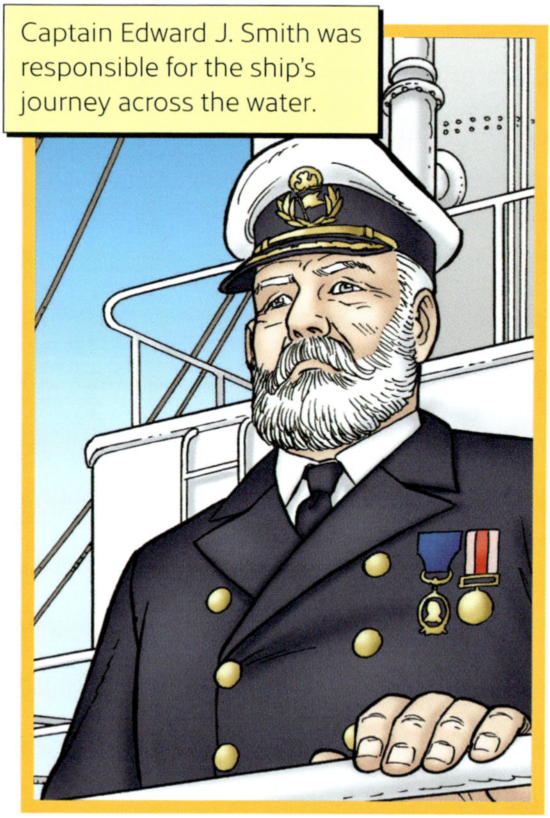
Captain Edward J. Smith was responsible for the ship's journey across the water.

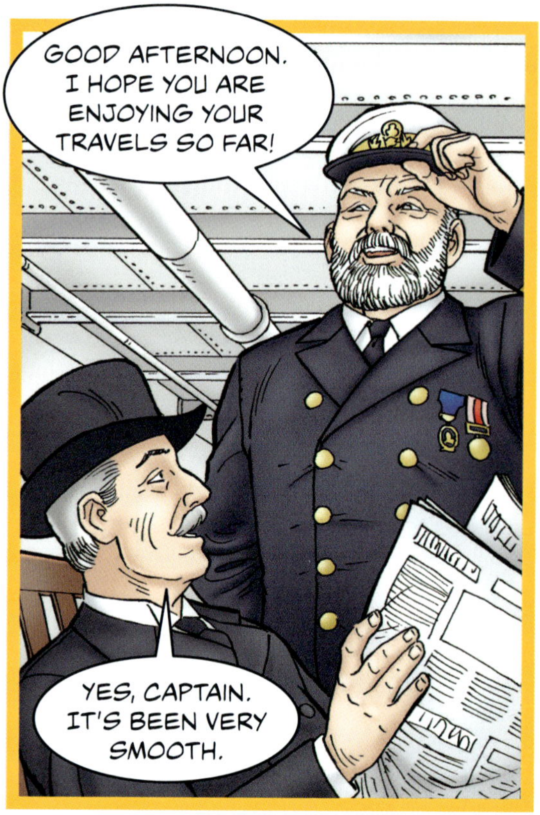
GOOD AFTERNOON. I HOPE YOU ARE ENJOYING YOUR TRAVELS SO FAR!
YES, CAPTAIN. IT'S BEEN VERY SMOOTH.

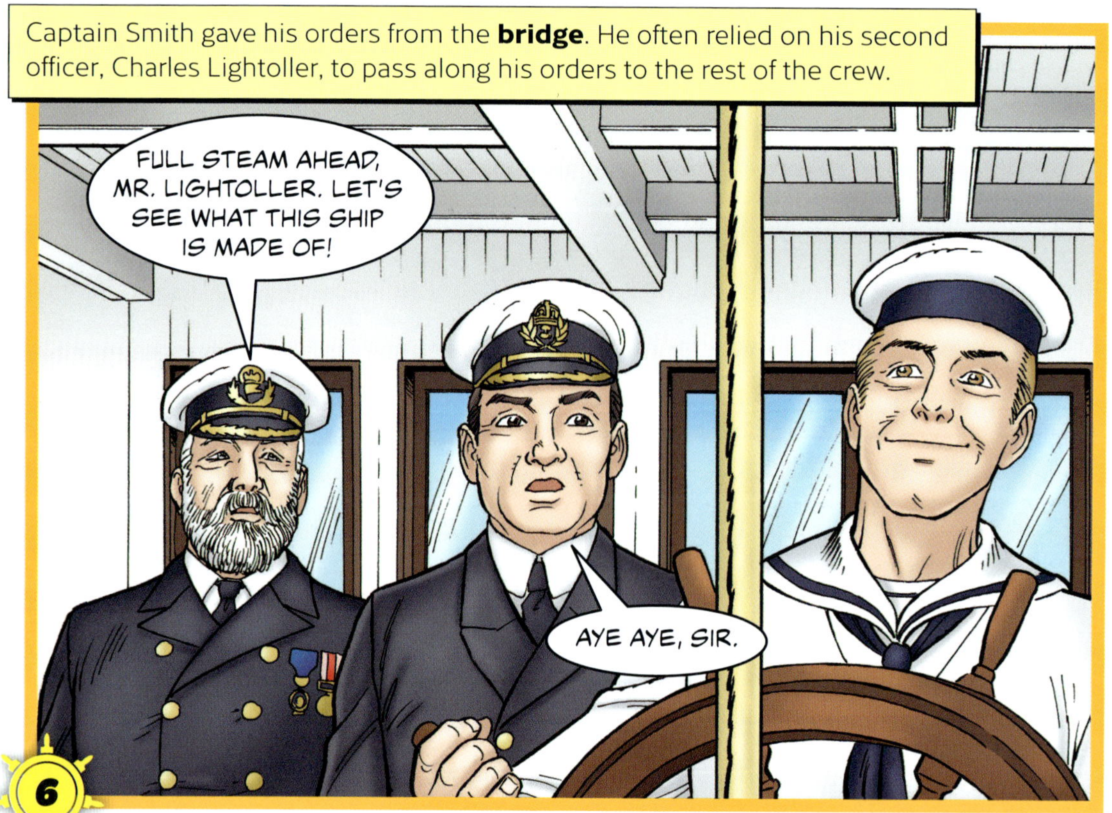
Captain Smith gave his orders from the **bridge**. He often relied on his second officer, Charles Lightoller, to pass along his orders to the rest of the crew.
FULL STEAM AHEAD, MR. LIGHTOLLER. LET'S SEE WHAT THIS SHIP IS MADE OF!
AYE AYE, SIR.

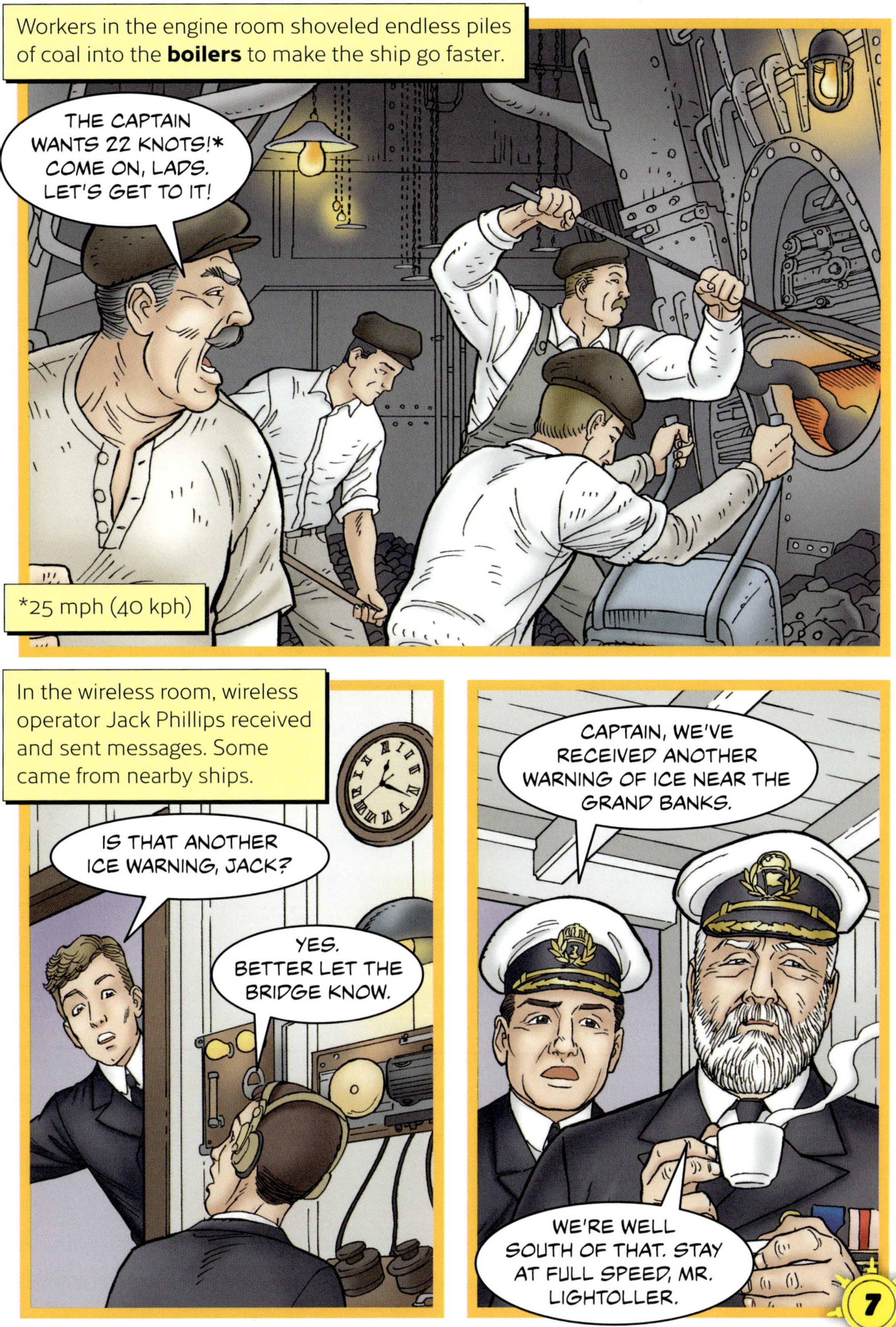
Workers in the engine room shoveled endless piles of coal into the **boilers** to make the ship go faster.
THE CAPTAIN WANTS 22 KNOTS!* COME ON, LADS. LET'S GET TO IT!
*25 mph (40 kph)
In the wireless room, wireless operator Jack Phillips received and sent messages. Some came from nearby ships.
IS THAT ANOTHER ICE WARNING, JACK?
YES. BETTER LET THE BRIDGE KNOW.
CAPTAIN, WE'VE RECEIVED ANOTHER WARNING OF ICE NEAR THE GRAND BANKS.
WE'RE WELL SOUTH OF THAT. STAY AT FULL SPEED, MR. LIGHTOLLER.

CHAPTER 2

Disaster Strikes

The journey was fine until the evening of April 14. At about 11:40 p.m., lookouts spotted a huge iceberg in the path of the ship.

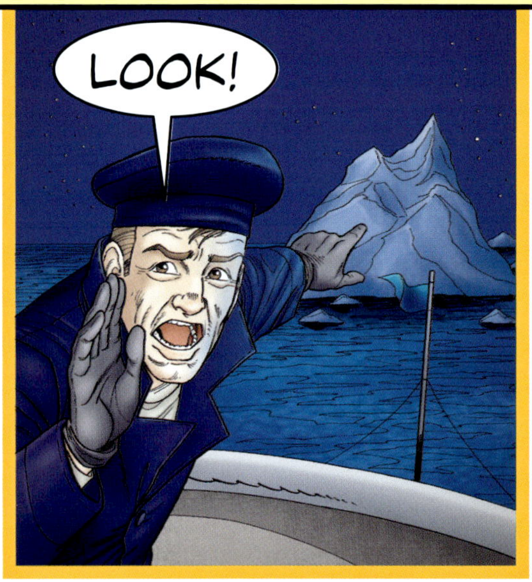

LOOK!

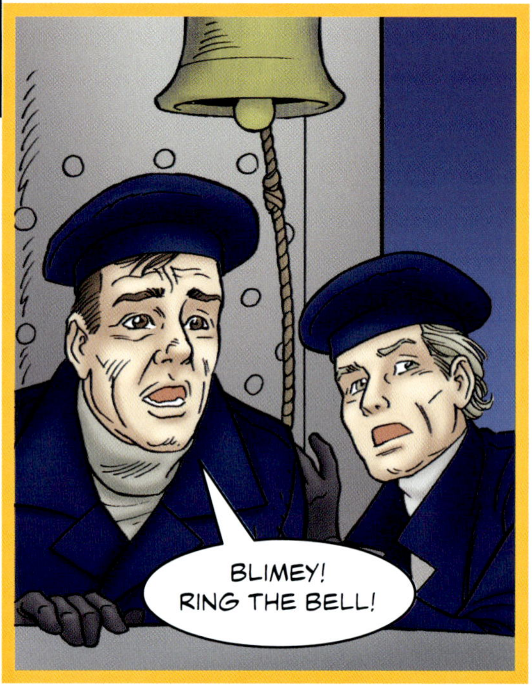

BLIMEY! RING THE BELL!

Lookout Frederick Fleet telephoned the bridge.

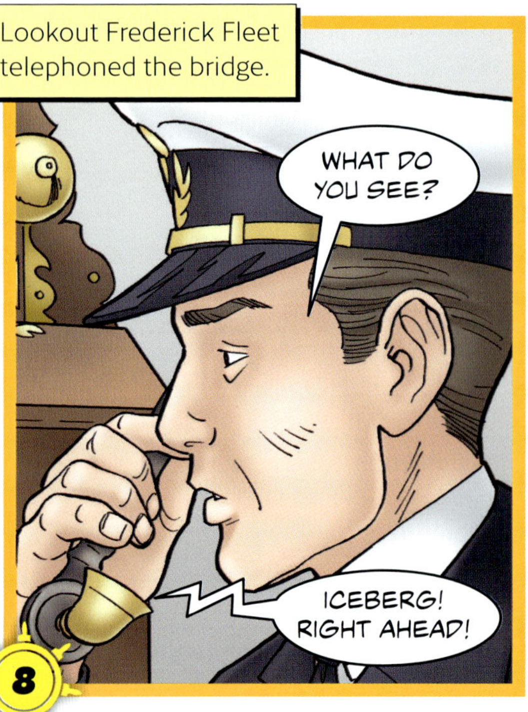

WHAT DO YOU SEE?
ICEBERG! RIGHT AHEAD!

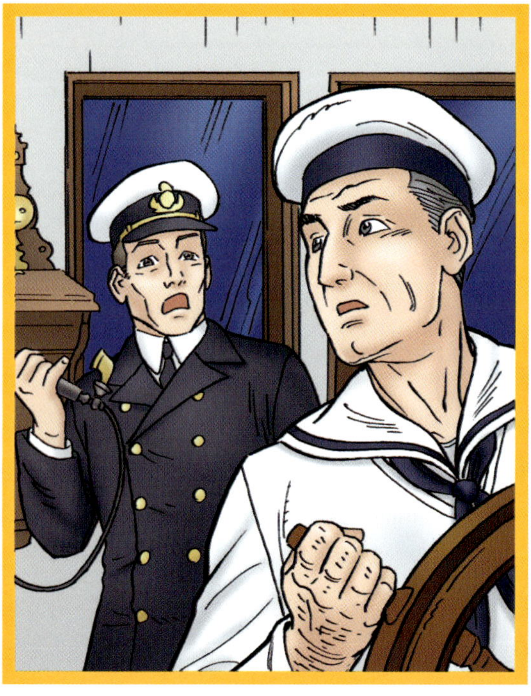

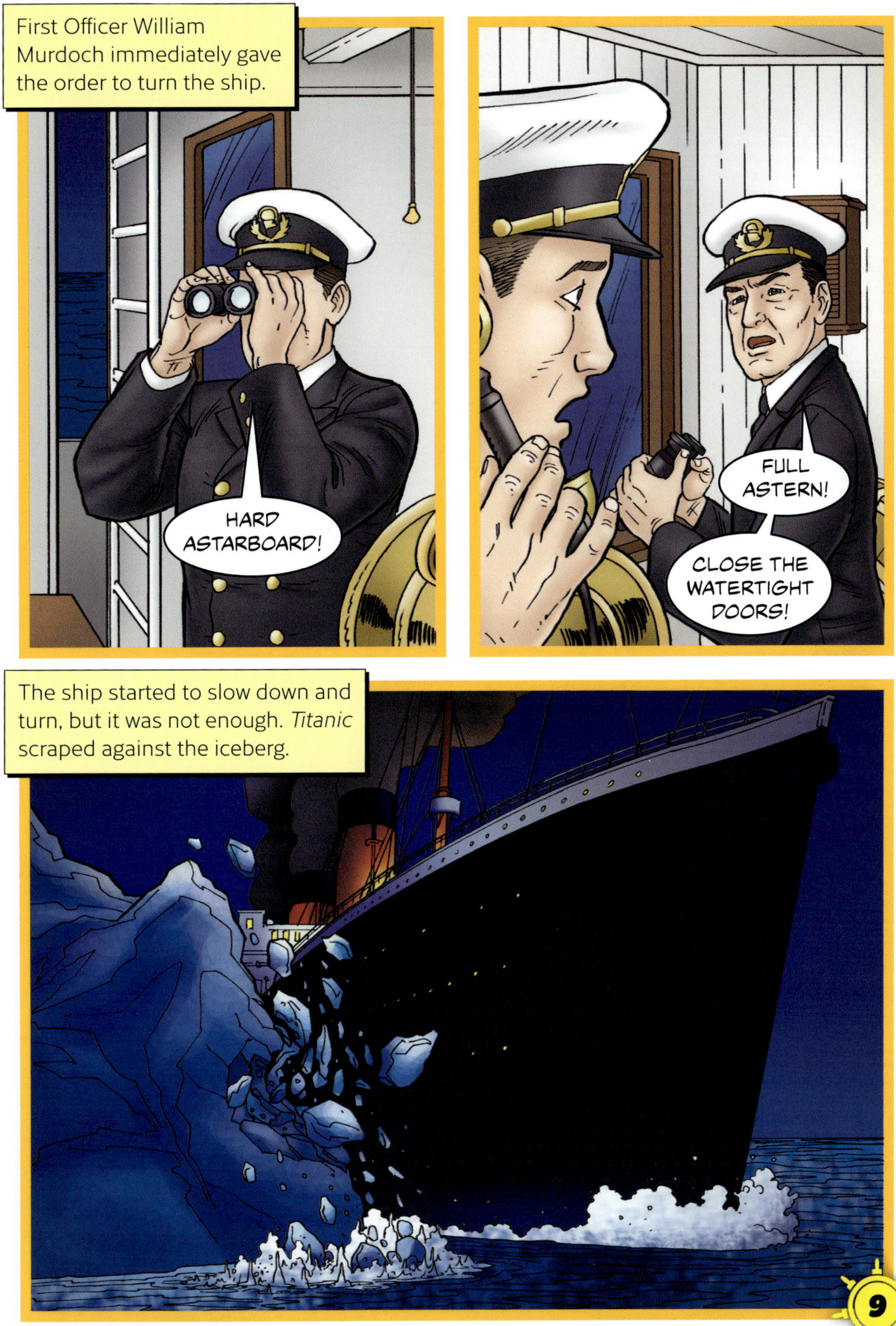
First Officer William Murdoch immediately gave the order to turn the ship.
HARD ASTARBOARD!
FULL ASTERN!
CLOSE THE WATERTIGHT DOORS!
The ship started to slow down and turn, but it was not enough. *Titanic* scraped against the iceberg.

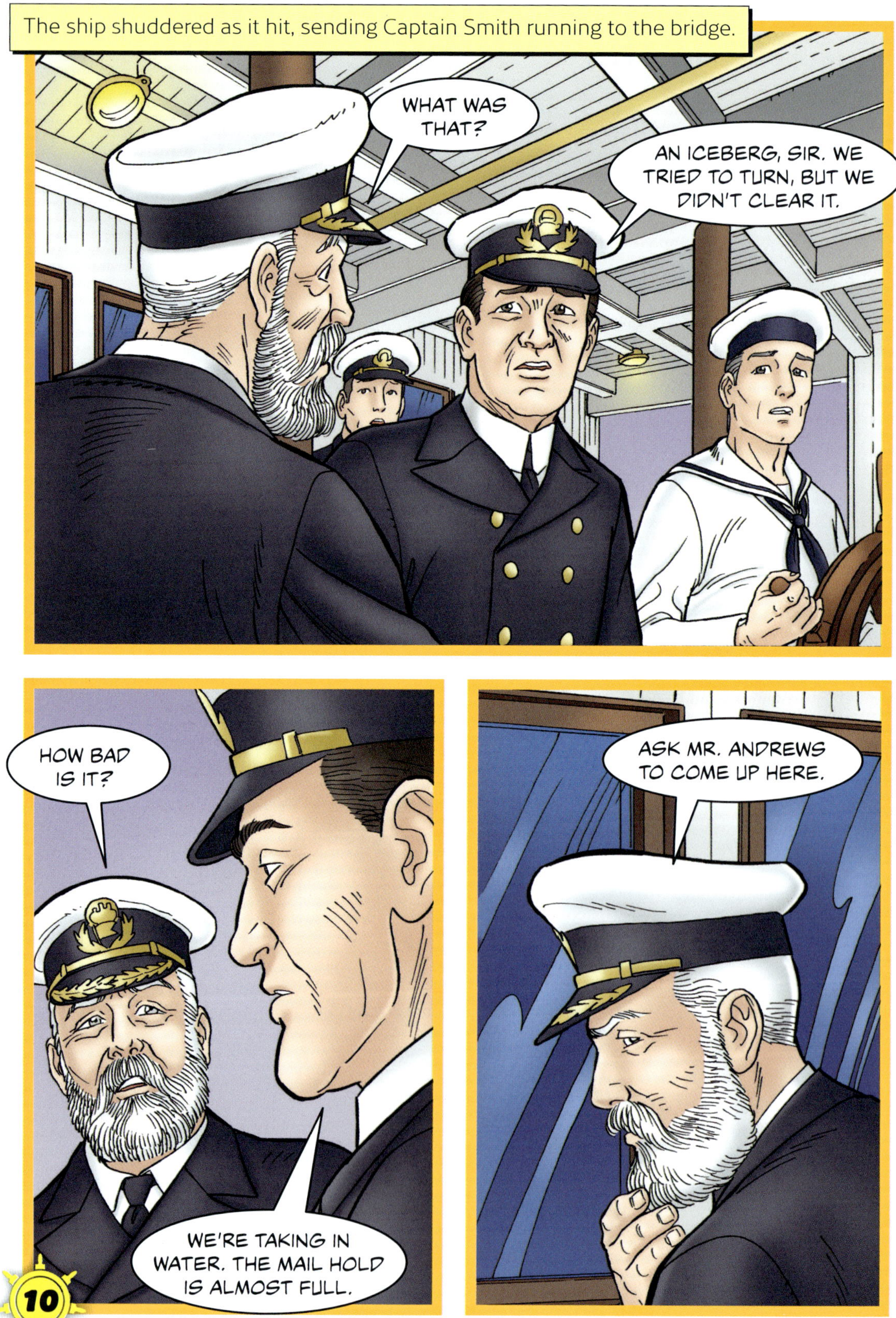
The ship shuddered as it hit, sending Captain Smith running to the bridge.
WHAT WAS THAT?
AN ICEBERG, SIR. WE TRIED TO TURN, BUT WE DIDN'T CLEAR IT.
HOW BAD IS IT?
WE'RE TAKING IN WATER. THE MAIL HOLD IS ALMOST FULL.
ASK MR. ANDREWS TO COME UP HERE.

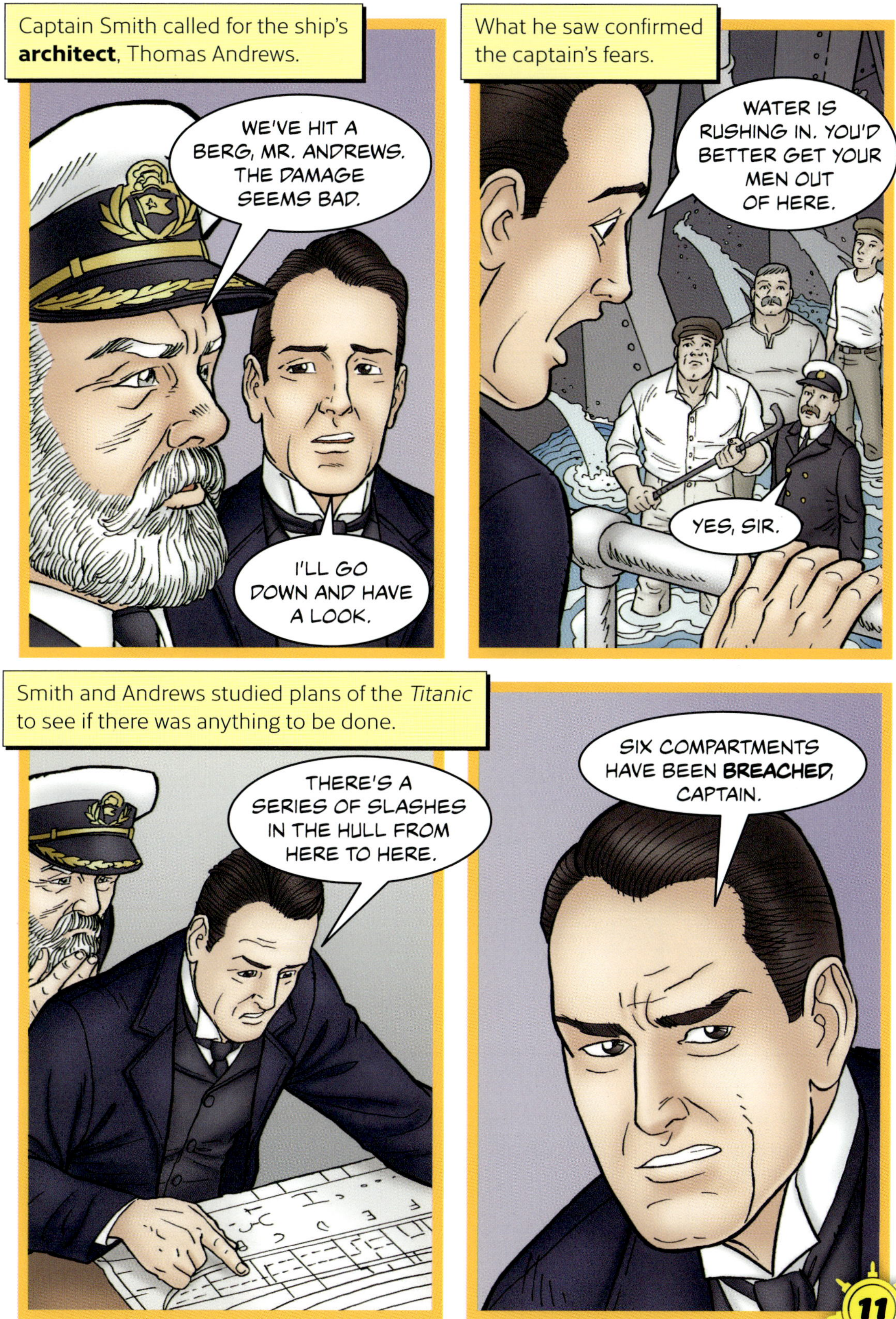
Captain Smith called for the ship's **architect**, Thomas Andrews.
WE'VE HIT A BERG, MR. ANDREWS. THE DAMAGE SEEMS BAD.
I'LL GO DOWN AND HAVE A LOOK.
What he saw confirmed the captain's fears.
WATER IS RUSHING IN. YOU'D BETTER GET YOUR MEN OUT OF HERE.
YES, SIR.
Smith and Andrews studied plans of the *Titanic* to see if there was anything to be done.
THERE'S A SERIES OF SLASHES IN THE HULL FROM HERE TO HERE.
SIX COMPARTMENTS HAVE BEEN **BREACHED**, CAPTAIN.

THE COMPARTMENT DOORS HAVE BEEN CLOSED TO CONTAIN THE WATER.
YES, BUT THE DOORS DON'T REACH TO THE CEILING. WATER WILL SPILL OVER THE TOP AND INTO FURTHER COMPARTMENTS.
IT WILL WEIGH THE SHIP DOWN AT THE **BOW**. I'M SORRY TO SAY THE *TITANIC* WILL SINK WITHIN HOURS.
READY THE LIFEBOATS!
Shortly after midnight, Second Officer Lightoller gathered some of the crew together.
ALL RIGHT, MEN. THE SHIP IS SERIOUSLY DAMAGED. START UNCOVERING THE LIFEBOATS.
BUT WE HAVEN'T BEEN PROPERLY TRAINED.

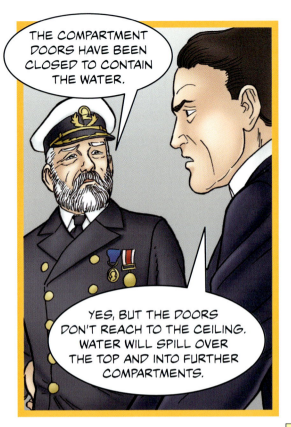

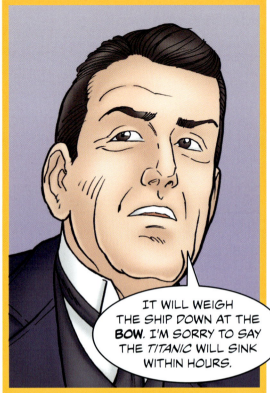

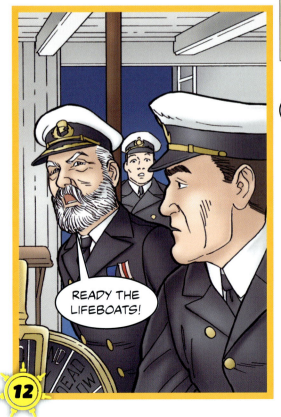

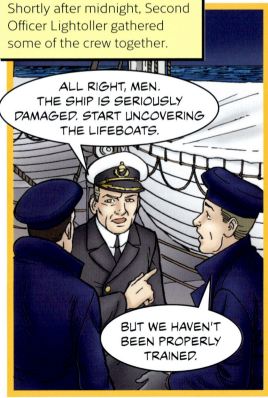

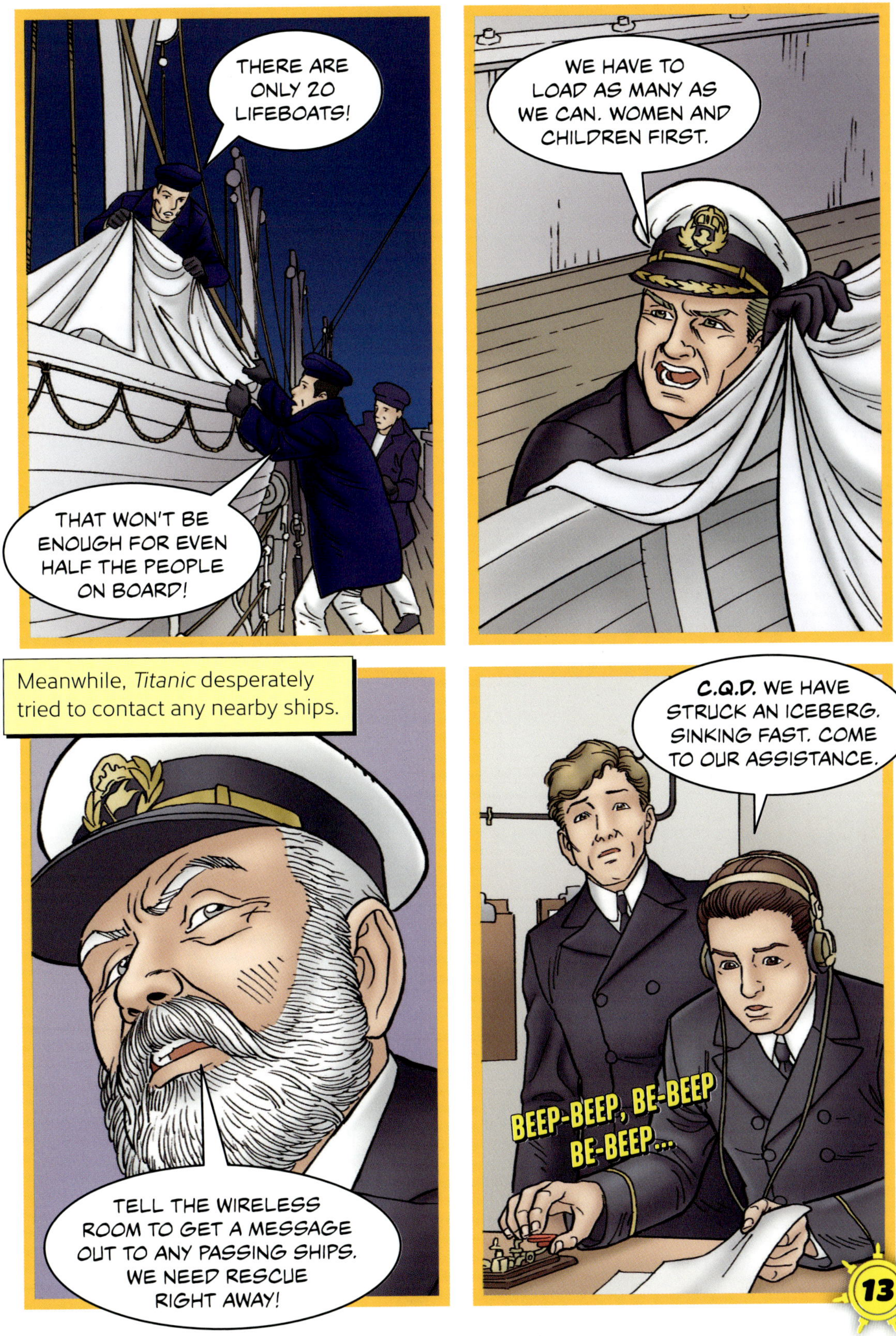
THERE ARE ONLY 20 LIFEBOATS!
THAT WON'T BE ENOUGH FOR EVEN HALF THE PEOPLE ON BOARD!
WE HAVE TO LOAD AS MANY AS WE CAN. WOMEN AND CHILDREN FIRST.
Meanwhile, *Titanic* desperately tried to contact any nearby ships.
TELL THE WIRELESS ROOM TO GET A MESSAGE OUT TO ANY PASSING SHIPS. WE NEED RESCUE RIGHT AWAY!
C.Q.D. WE HAVE STRUCK AN ICEBERG. SINKING FAST. COME TO OUR ASSISTANCE.
BEEP-BEEP, BE-BEEP BE-BEEP...

CHAPTER 3

Nightmare at Sea

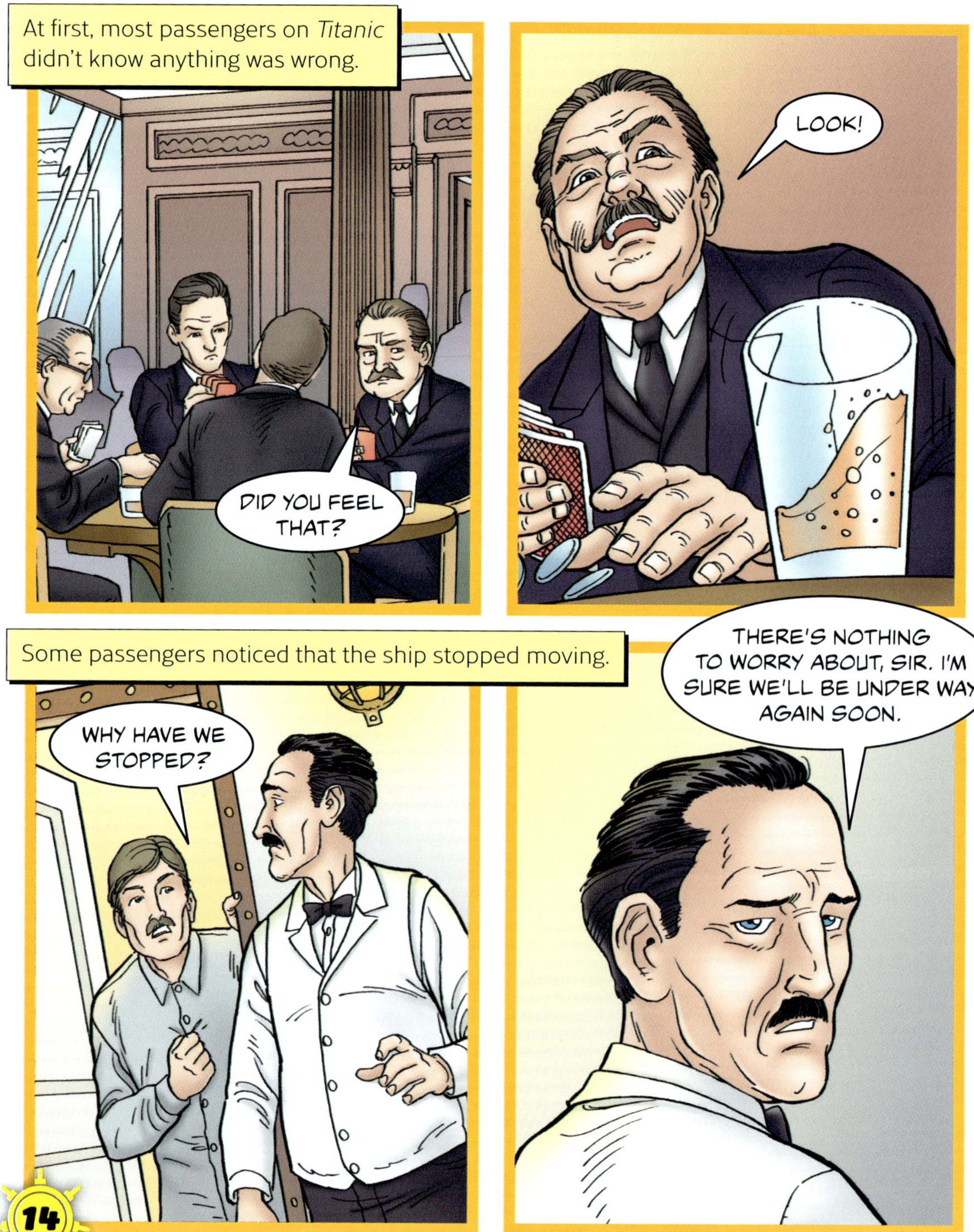
At first, most passengers on *Titanic* didn't know anything was wrong.
DID YOU FEEL THAT?
LOOK!
Some passengers noticed that the ship stopped moving.
WHY HAVE WE STOPPED?
THERE'S NOTHING TO WORRY ABOUT, SIR. I'M SURE WE'LL BE UNDER WAY AGAIN SOON.

There were even passengers who found fun in the immediate **aftermath** of impact.

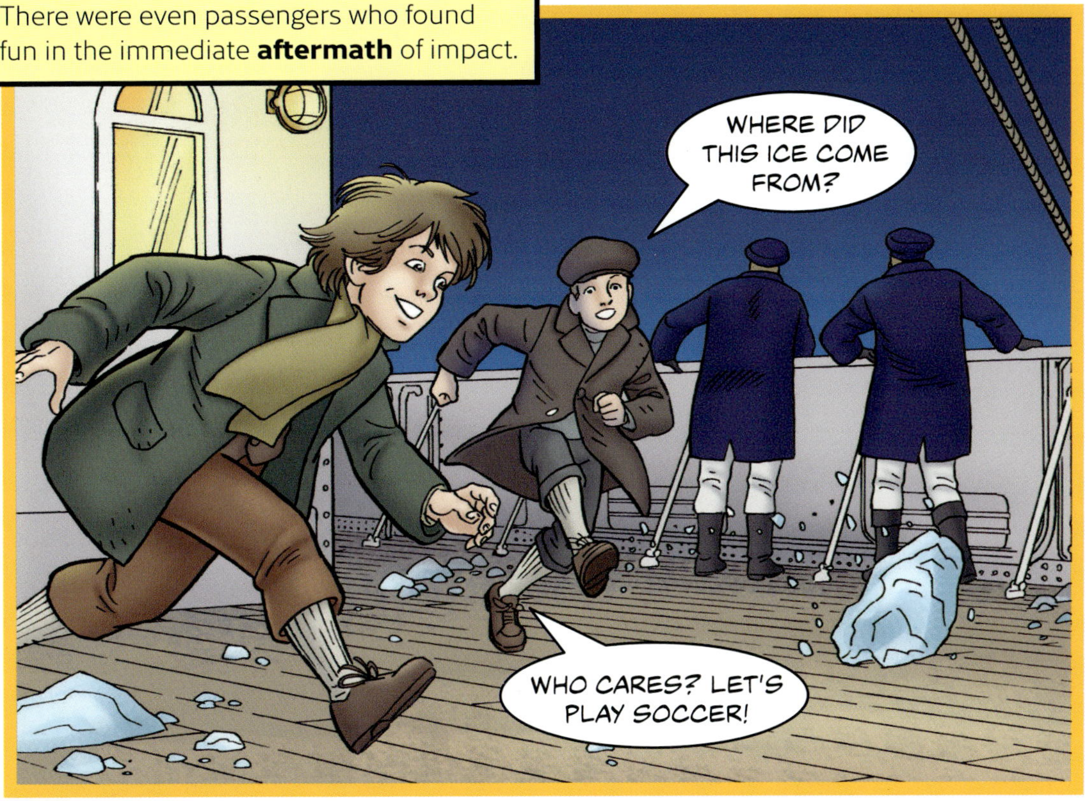
WHERE DID THIS ICE COME FROM?
WHO CARES? LET'S PLAY SOCCER!

At around 12:30 a.m., crew members began telling passengers to put on life jackets. But some passengers still didn't realize the danger.

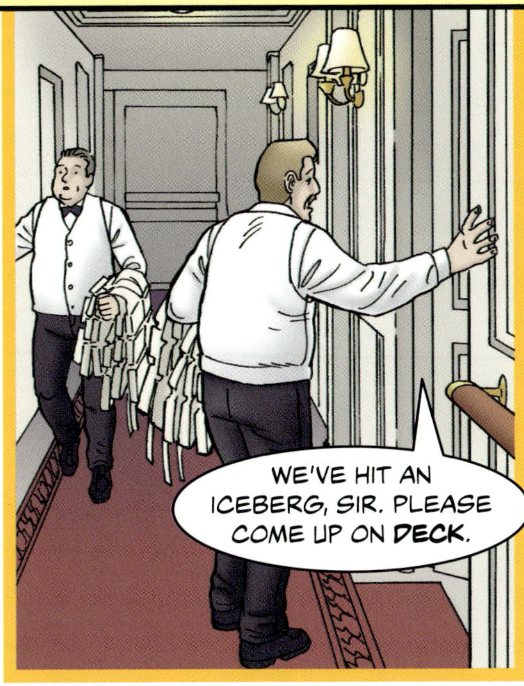
WE'VE HIT AN ICEBERG, SIR. PLEASE COME UP ON **DECK**.

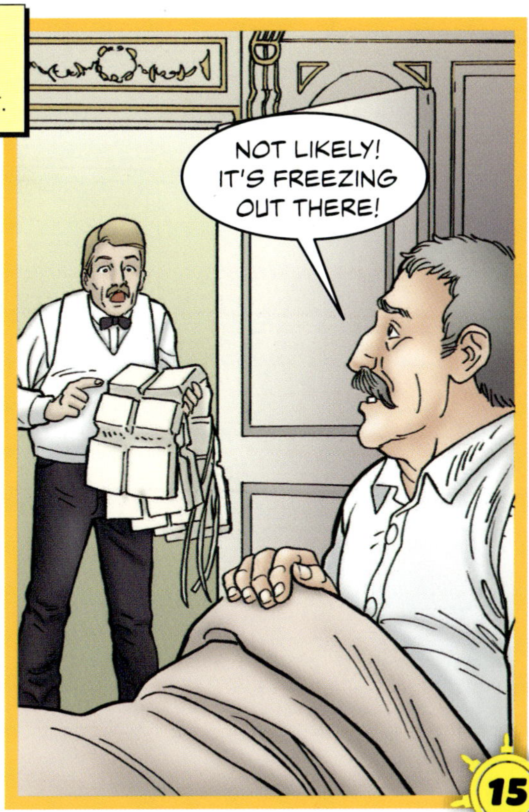
NOT LIKELY! IT'S FREEZING OUT THERE!

The crew was told to keep passengers calm. Many aboard *Titanic* never dreamed the boat was going under.

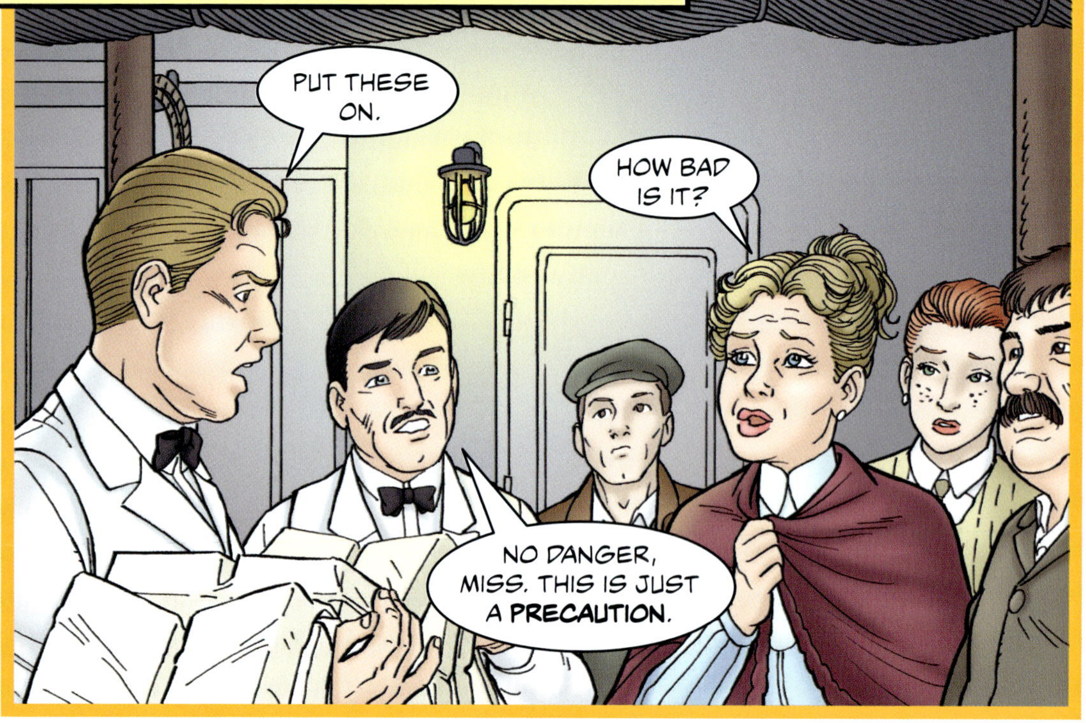
PUT THESE ON.
HOW BAD IS IT?
NO DANGER, MISS. THIS IS JUST A **PRECAUTION**.

Even as the first lifeboat was ready to be launched, many refused to get on.

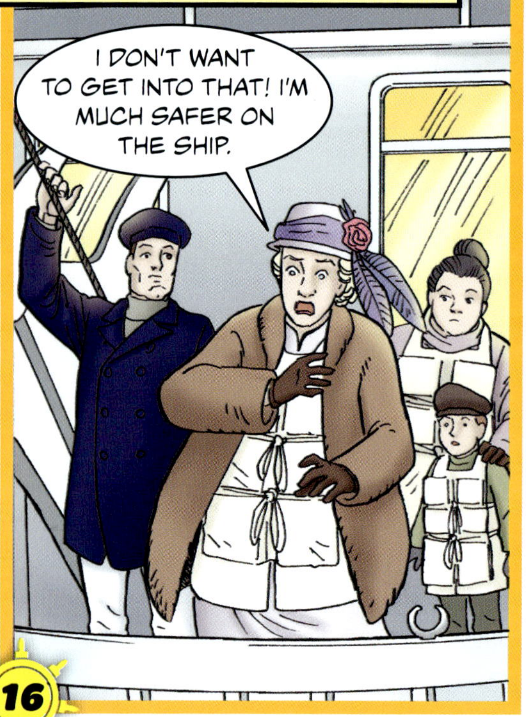
I DON'T WANT TO GET INTO THAT! I'M MUCH SAFER ON THE SHIP.

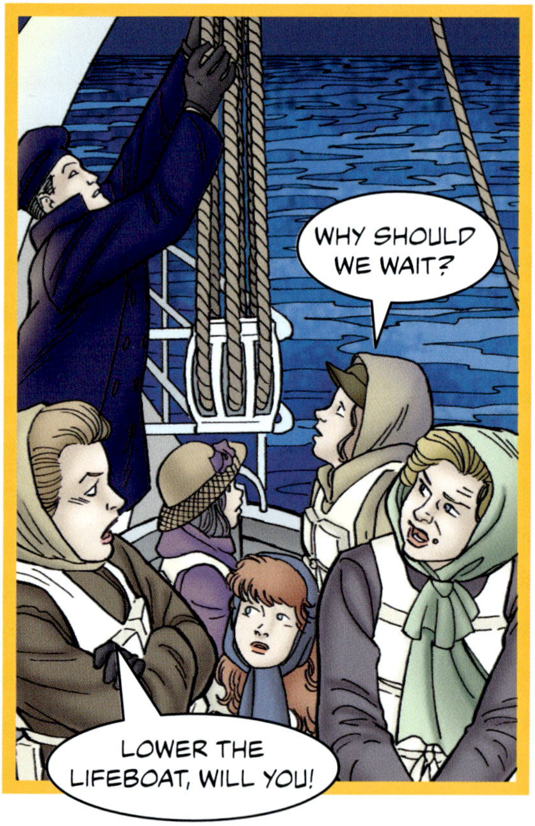
WHY SHOULD WE WAIT?
LOWER THE LIFEBOAT, WILL YOU!

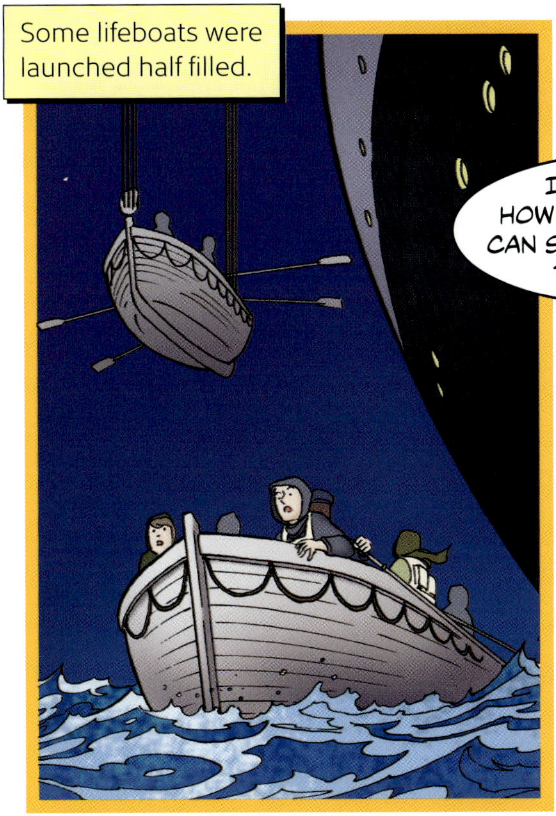
Some lifeboats were launched half filled.

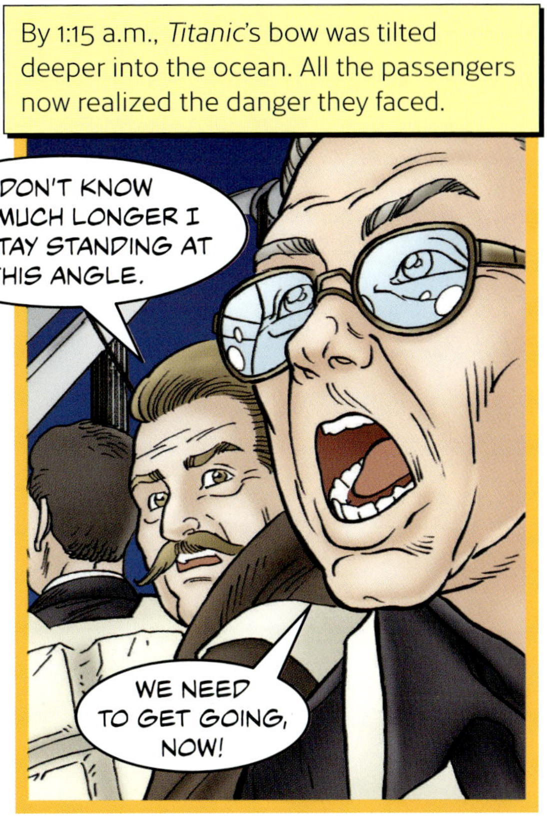
By 1:15 a.m., *Titanic*'s bow was tilted deeper into the ocean. All the passengers now realized the danger they faced.
I DON'T KNOW HOW MUCH LONGER I CAN STAY STANDING AT THIS ANGLE.
WE NEED TO GET GOING, NOW!

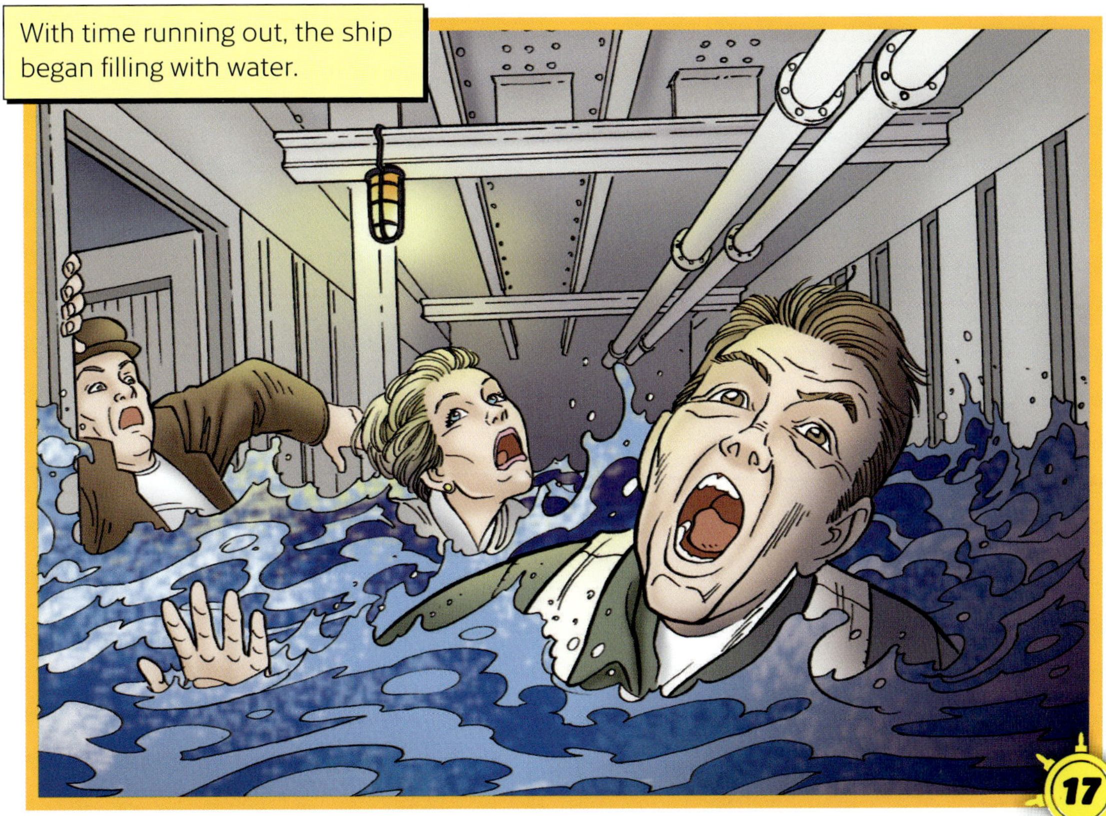
With time running out, the ship began filling with water.

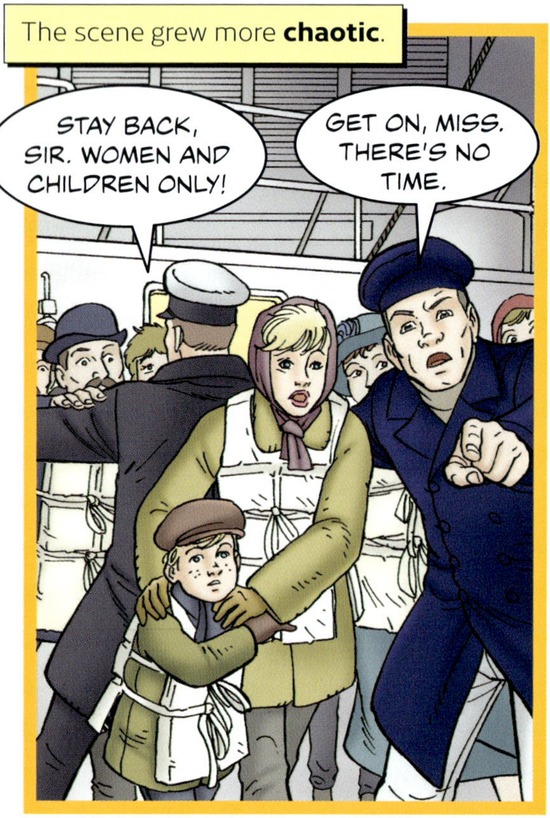
The scene grew more **chaotic**.
STAY BACK, SIR. WOMEN AND CHILDREN ONLY!
GET ON, MISS. THERE'S NO TIME.

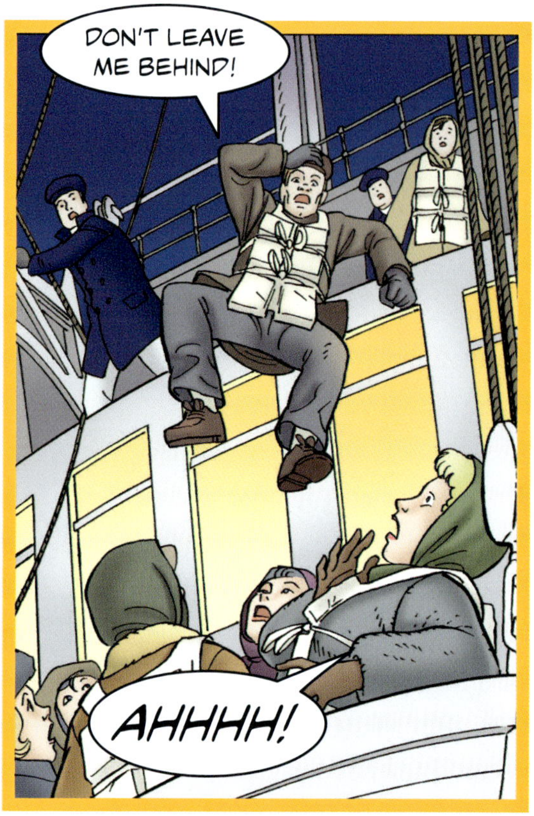
DON'T LEAVE ME BEHIND!
AHHHH!

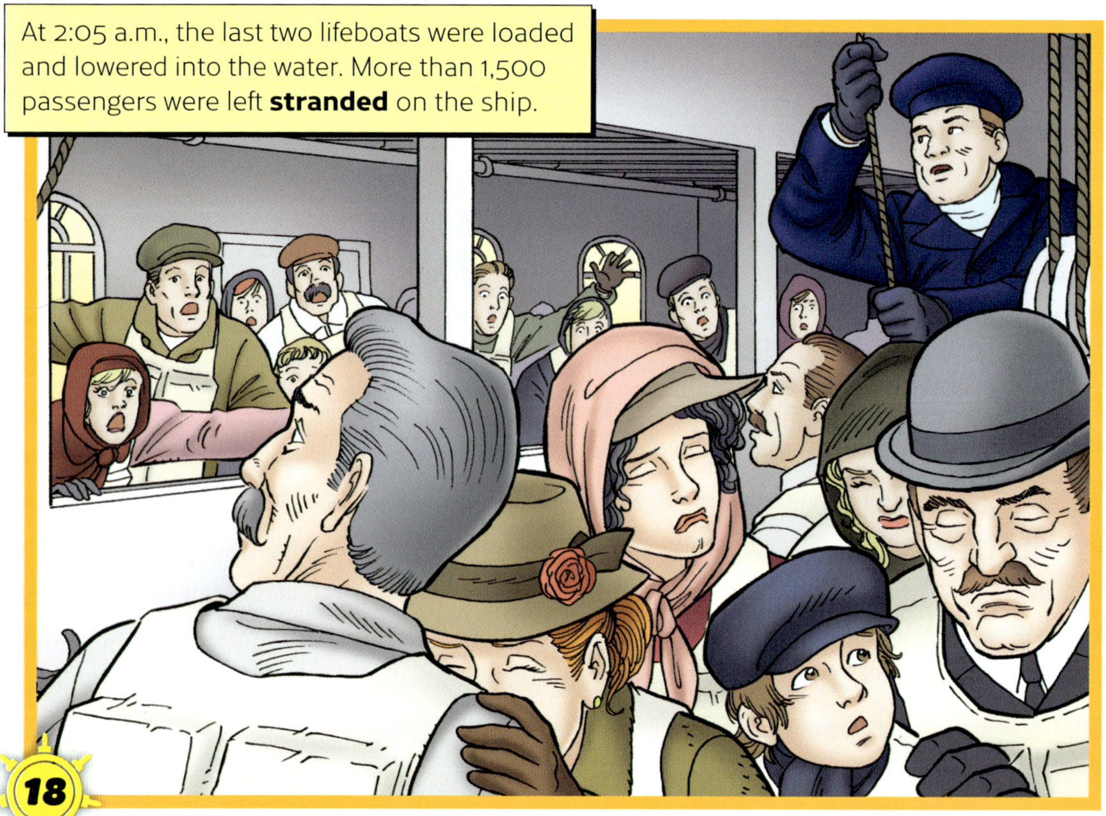
At 2:05 a.m., the last two lifeboats were loaded and lowered into the water. More than 1,500 passengers were left **stranded** on the ship.

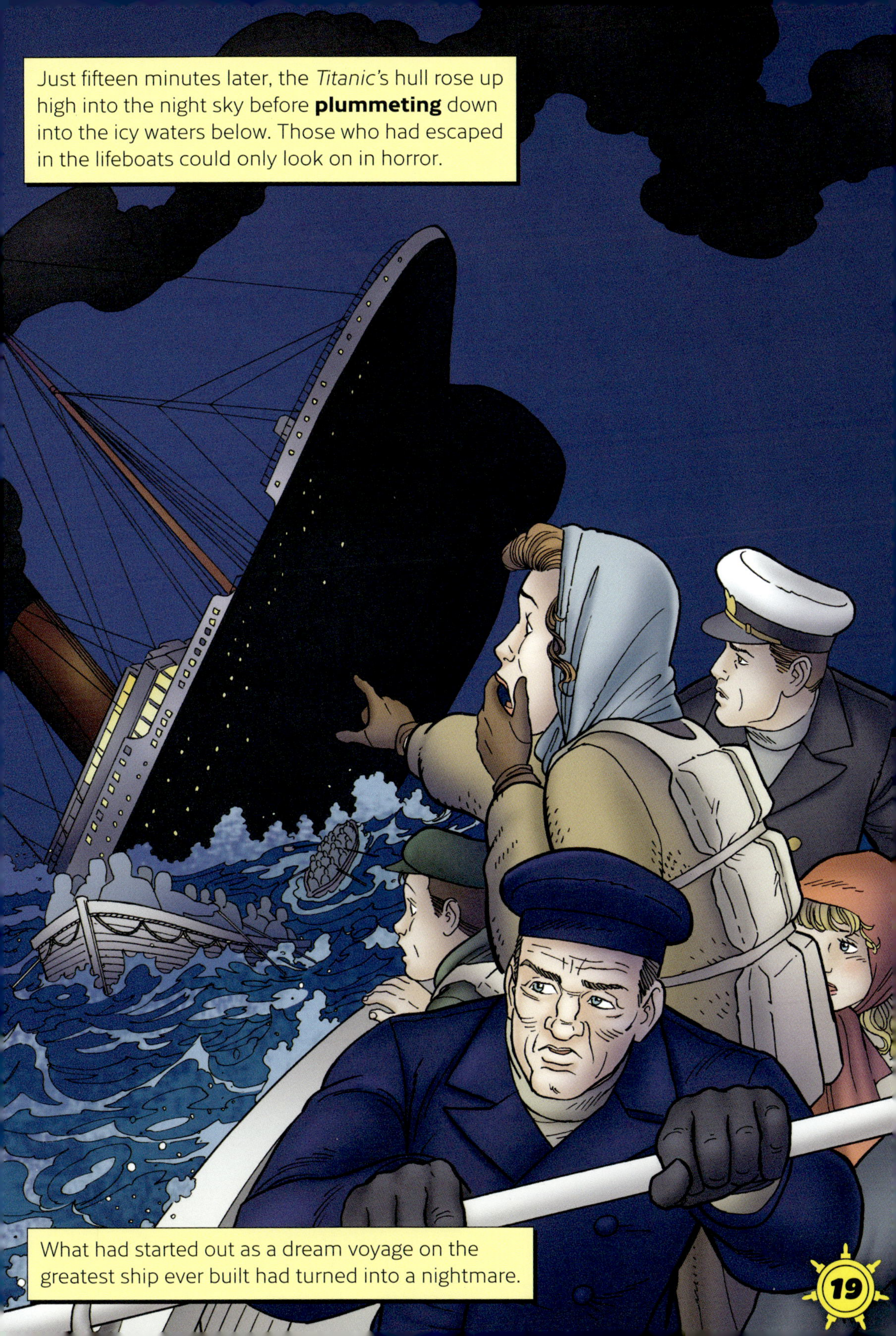
Just fifteen minutes later, the *Titanic*'s hull rose up high into the night sky before **plummeting** down into the icy waters below. Those who had escaped in the lifeboats could only look on in horror.
What had started out as a dream voyage on the greatest ship ever built had turned into a nightmare.

The Sinking of the *Titanic*

When *Titanic* struck the iceberg, the ice cut small gashes in the right front side of the ship. Water rushed in, flooding the mail room and one of the boiler rooms. Although the crew shut the compartment doors, water began to flow over the tall walls. Before long, another four compartments were filling with water. The ship's architect, Thomas Andrews, knew the ship would sink if more than four compartments were flooded.

Soon, the water began to weigh down the ship's bow. The engine crew worked hard to keep the ship's lights going so passengers and crew could see as they launched the lifeboats. Telegraph operators sent emergency messages to other ships in the area. Although three ships said they would come, they were several hours away. The crew tried desperately to reach anybody closer. They stayed on board the sinking ship, sending messages up through the *Titanic*'s last minutes above the water.

A REPLICA OF *TITANIC*'S WIRELESS ROOM

As the ship filled with water, its stern rose high into the air. This put great strain on the middle of the ship and *Titanic* broke in two. Shortly after, both halves disappeared beneath the waves.

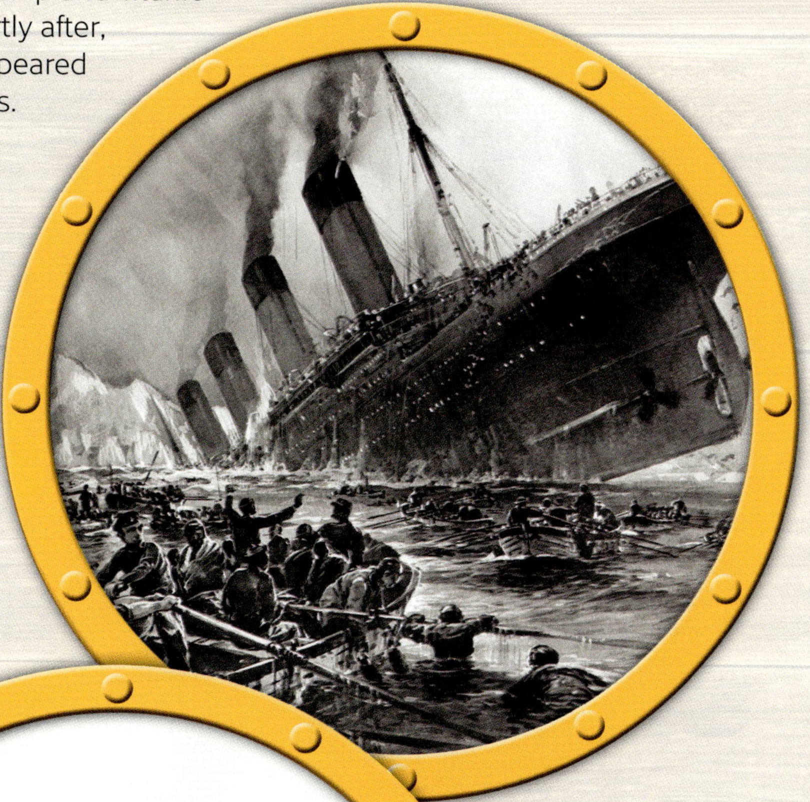

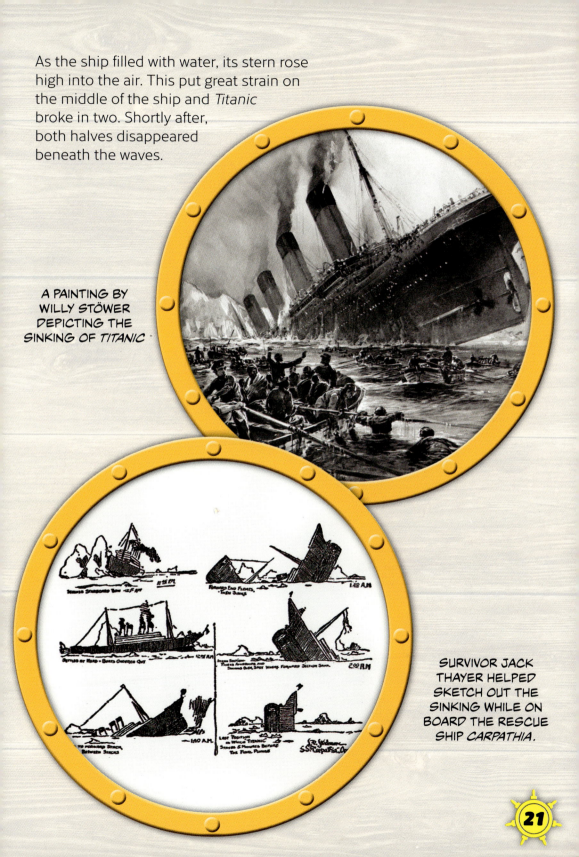

A PAINTING BY WILLY STÖWER DEPICTING THE SINKING OF *TITANIC*

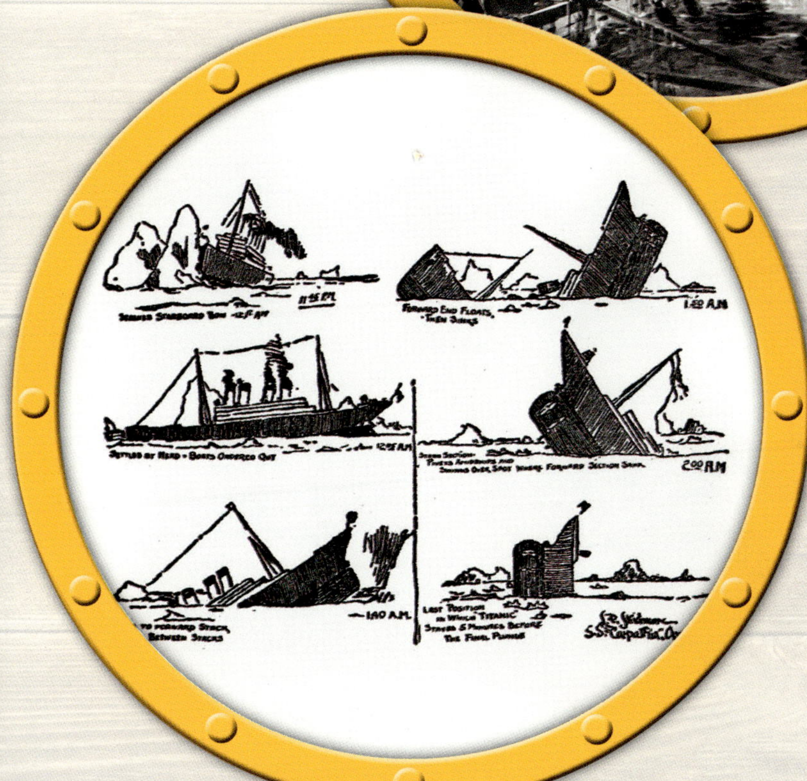
11.45 P.M.
Forward End Floats, Then Sinks
1.40 A.M.
Settled by Head - Boats Ordered Out
12.45 A.M.
2.00 A.M.
1.40 A.M.
Between Stacks
Last Position in Which Titanic Stayed 5 Minutes Before The Final Plunge
S.S. Carpathia

SURVIVOR JACK THAYER HELPED SKETCH OUT THE SINKING WHILE ON BOARD THE RESCUE SHIP *CARPATHIA*.

More Titanic Stories

The Goldsmith family were third-class passengers on *Titanic*. They were traveling to join relatives in Michigan, in the hope of a better life. Frank Goldsmith felt the shudder of the collision and woke his wife Emily and their 10-year-old son Frankie. Frankie and Emily made it onto a lifeboat. They were rescued two hours later by RMS *Carpathia*. Unfortunately, Frank went down with the ship. When Frankie died almost 70 years later, his ashes were scattered in the place where *Titanic* sank so son could be reunited with father.

THE GOLDSMITH FAMILY

JACK PHILLIPS

Jack Phillips was *Titanic*'s senior telegraph operator. On April 14, Jack and his assistant Harold Bride were working through a backlog of passenger messages. As they were sending out the messages, they were also receiving ice warnings from nearby ships. When disaster struck, Jack sent out distress calls and shared *Titanic*'s position. Although he knew the ship would sink, he remained at his post. Jack's bravery helped to save lives. His last message was cut off when the ship's power failed, minutes before *Titanic* sank.

Glossary

aftermath the period immediately following an event

architect a person who designs buildings or other large objects

boilers parts of an engine that make steam to produce power

bow the front end of a ship

breached broken through

bridge the part of a ship from which the captain and officers control the ship

chaotic a state of complete confusion

C.Q.D. a distress signal used in the 1910s, later replaced by S.O.S.

deck the floor of a ship or boat, especially the upper, open level

luxuries expensive items or services that are desirable but not essential

opulent showing great wealth

plummeting falling down suddenly

precaution care taken in advance

steerage the third-class portion of a ship

stranded left behind or stuck

HEARINGS INVESTIGATING *TITANIC*'S SINKING BEGAN ON APRIL 19, 1912, AT THE WALDORF-ASTORIA HOTEL IN NEW YORK CITY.

Index

Andrews, Thomas 10–11, 20
boiler room 20
crew 6, 12, 15–16, 20
first-class passengers 4
Goldsmith family 22
iceberg 8–10, 13, 15, 20
lifeboats 12–13, 16–20, 22
life jackets 15
Smith, Captain Edward 6, 10–11
telegraph 20, 22
third-class passengers 5, 22

Read More

Lassieur, Allison. *Facing Tragedy on the* Titanic*: An Interactive Look at History (You Choose: Seeking History).* North Mankato, MN: Capstone Press, 2024.

McClure Anastasia, Laura. *Four Days on the* Titanic *(A True Book).* New York: Scholastic Inc., 2022.

O'Daly, Anne. *Sunken Ship of Dreams! The* Titanic, *1912 (Doomed History).* Minneapolis: Bearport Publishing Company, 2022.

Learn More Online

1. Go to **FactSurfer.com** or scan the QR code below.
2. Enter "**Disaster Strikes**" into the search box.
3. Click on the cover of this book to see a list of websites.